The Usborne Book of

First Experiences

Anne Civardi

Illustrated by Stephen Cartwright

Edited by Michelle Bates

Cover design by Hannah Ahmed

Contents

There is a little yellow duck hiding on every page. Can you find it?

Note for Parents

Children's experiences in hospitals will vary according to where you are and what the operation is. We've chosen to use gas for the anaesthetic but other methods are often used. To help prepare your child as much as possible you could ask the surgeon to explain what sort of anaesthetic your child is likely to be given and use this information in conjunction with this book.

Going to the hospit

Medical adviser: Catherine Sims BS
American consultant: Dr. Lance Ki

Ben is s
His ear

2

This is the Bell family.

Mr. Bell

Jack and Jill

Mrs. Bell

Ben Bell

Bess Bell

Simba

...ix and Bess is three. Ben is not feeling very well. ...ches. His ear often aches and it hurts a lot.

Mrs. Bell takes Ben to see Doctor Small.

Doctor Small looks in Ben's ear with an auroscope. He says that Ben needs to have an operation on his sore ear.

Ben has to go to the hospital.

There are lots of other children around. Mrs. Bell helps
Ben change his clothes and unpack his suitcase.

He will have his operation later today. He isn't allowed to eat anything for six hours before it.

Ben meets the nurse.

She tucks him up in bed. She takes his temperature and pulse to make sure they are normal.

Then she checks his blood pressure with a special machine. She writes down the results on Ben's chart.

The surgeon comes to see Ben.

She is going to operate on Ben's ear. She tells him what she is going to do, and listens to his heartbeat with a stethoscope.

Ben is ready for his operation.

The nurse comes in to see how Ben is before he is taken
to the operating room.

Ben is taken for his operation.

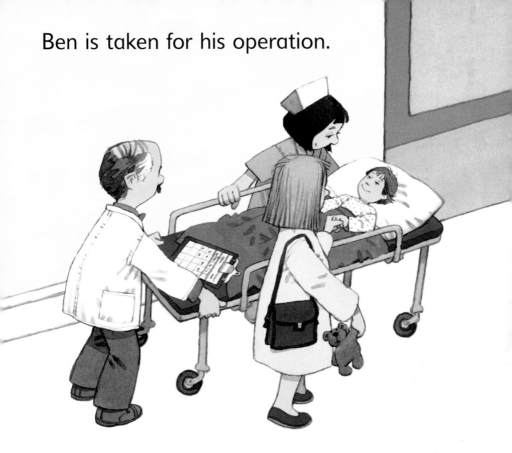

He is wheeled down the long corridors to the operating room. The nurse and Mrs. Bell go with him.

Ben breathes in some gas.

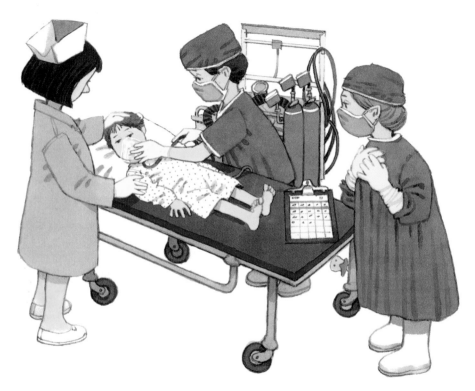

The gas is an anaesthetic which makes Ben sleep soundly during his operation. He has more gas during the operation.

Ben's operation is over.

Ben is taken back to his room. He is still sleepy, but he is pleased to see his mother waiting for him.

Ben goes to the play area.

Ben's ear feels a bit sore, but he feels well enough to get out of bed and play with the other children.

Ben eats lots.

He is very hungry because he hasn't had anything to eat since breakfast.

Ben's family comes to visit him.

Ben is very pleased to see his family, especially his Granny.
Ben shows her his ear. He is very proud of his bandage.

Granny says Ben has been a brave boy and gives him a new toy car. The other children have visitors too.

Ben is ready to go home.

His earache has gone. He says goodbye to the nurse and the surgeon and gives them a big bunch of flowers.

Going to the doctor

Medical adviser: Catherine Sims BSc; MBBS and Dr. Lance King

This is the Jay family.

Mrs. Jay

Mr. Jay

Jack Jay

Jenny Jay

Joey Jay

Nod

Rory

Jenny has woken up with a bad cough and Jack has hurt his arm. They must go and see the doctor.

Mrs. Jay phones the doctor.

She makes an appointment while Mr. Jay helps Jack get dressed. "Ow," shouts Jack, "watch my arm, Dad."

The Jays go to see the doctor.

Mrs. Jay takes Jack, Jenny and Joey to see Doctor Woody.
"We've an appointment at 2 o'clock," she tells the receptionist.

The receptionist checks her book.

"Yes, it's for Jack and Jenny, isn't it?" she says. "And for Joey too," says Mrs. Jay. "He needs to have his immunization."

The Jays sit in the waiting room.

There are lots of people waiting to see the doctor. Mrs. Jay reads a book to Jenny. Jack and Joey want to play.

Now it is the Jays' turn.

Doctor Woody calls their name. "Who shall I see first?"
she says. "Me," says Jack, holding out his arm.

Doctor Woody examines Jack.

She looks at his sore arm. "It's not broken," she says, "but you do have a sprained wrist, Jack."

Doctor Woody puts Jack's arm in a sling.

"Just wear this for a few days," Doctor Woody tells him.
"It will feel better soon."

Doctor Woody checks Jenny.

She takes her temperature with a thermometer. Then she looks down Jenny's throat. "It's very red," she says.

Then she examines Jenny's ears with an auroscope. "Your ears are fine," she tells Jenny.

Doctor Woody listens to Jenny's breathing with a stethoscope. "Breathe in and out deeply," she says.

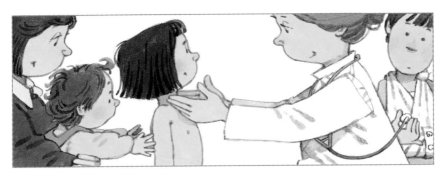

She feels Jenny's neck to see if her glands are swollen. "You have a slight chest infection," she says.

Jenny needs some medicine.

Doctor Woody prints a prescription for Jenny from her computer. Then she sits down at her desk and signs it.

Now it is Joey's turn.

Doctor Woody gives Joey his immunization. It only hurts a little.

She also gives Joey some drops so that he won't get polio. Then she says goodbye to the Jays.

The Jays pick up Jenny's prescription.

Mrs. Jay stops at the pharmacy. She gives the pharmacist the prescription and he gives her some medicine.

At home, Mrs. Jay puts Jenny to bed.

Mrs. Jay tucks Jenny in and gives her a spoonful of
medicine. "You'll be better soon," she says.

That evening, Mr. Jay comes home from work.

"How are you all?" he says. Jack jumps to his feet. "Joey's all right, and Jenny's in bed," he says. "But look at my sling!"

Going to school

This is the Peach family.

Mrs. Peach

Mr. Peach

Polly Peach

Pong the kitten

Percy Peach

Sidney the gerbil

Ping the other kitten

Dusty the cat

Percy and Polly are twins. Tomorrow they are going to school for the first time.

This is where the Peaches live.

They live above the Marsh family. Millie Marsh is going to the same school as the twins.

Mr. and Mrs. Peach wake Percy and Polly.

It is 8 o'clock in the morning. It is time for them to get
ready for school. Percy and Polly get up and get dressed.

They have their breakfast.

Then the twins put on their shoes and coats. Millie is ready to go to school with them.

They all go to school.

At first, Polly is a little shy. Mrs. Todd, the teacher, says that Mrs. Peach can stay with her for a while.

Mr. Peach hangs Percy's coat on his own special hook. He has to take Percy's pet gerbil, Sidney, back home with him.

Percy and Polly join their class.

There are lots of things to do at school such as painting, drawing, reading and dressing-up.

40

Some children make things out of paper, and others make things with clay. What are Percy and Polly doing?

They have fun making things.

Two of the teachers help them make tiny washing lines
full of clothes to take home.

It's time for singing.

Miss Dot, the music teacher, teaches them lots of songs.
She also teaches them how to play lots of instruments.

Now it's time for a break.

At 11 o'clock, everyone has a drink and something to eat.
Percy and Polly are both very thirsty.

It's story time.

Mrs. Todd tells the children a story about a big tiger named Stripes. What is Percy up to now?

The children go out to the playground.

There are lots of things to play with outside. There are tractors and hoops, and bicycles and balls.

Polly loves going down the slide. Percy likes to play in the sand. But Millie has found something else to play with.

47

It's time for Percy and Polly to go home.

They have had a happy day at school and so has Millie.
They have made lots of new friends.

Going to the dentist

This is the Judd family.

Mr. Judd

Mrs. Judd

Jake Judd

Jessie Judd

Jasper

Jake and Jessie need to have a check-up with their dentist.
Mr. Judd phones to make an appointment.

A few days later, they go to see the dentist.

Mrs. Judd takes Jake and Jessie in her car. Jasper goes too, but he won't be allowed to go in with them.

The dentist is very busy.

There are lots of people waiting to see him. Jake and Jessie play in the waiting room until it is their turn.

Jake and Jessie meet the dental nurse.

She calls them in to see the dentist. She is going to help with Jake and Jessie's check-up.

"Hello Jake, hello Jessie," says the dentist.

"Hello," say Jake and Jessie. The dentist says that Mrs. Judd can come in and watch.

Jessie goes first.

The dental nurse puts a bib around Jessie's neck. Then Jessie sits in a special chair that can go up and down.

Jessie has her teeth checked.

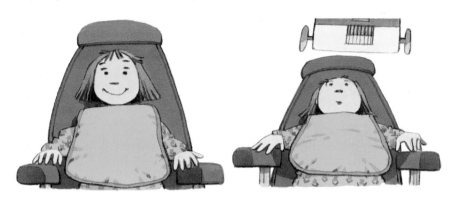

There is a spotlight above Jessie which shines into her mouth.

The dentist wears special gloves and a mask over his nose and mouth. He puts the chair back before he checks Jessie's teeth.

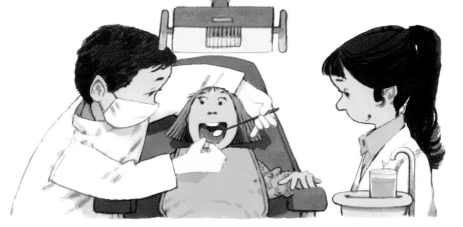

Jessie opens her mouth wide. He uses a mirror to see inside.

The dentist looks at each of Jessie's teeth. The dental nurse writes down notes about them.

The dentist has finished with Jessie.

He is very pleased with her. Jessie has no holes in her teeth. Now she can rinse out her mouth.

Now it is Jake's turn.

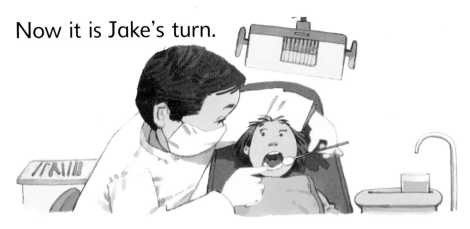

When the dentist checks Jake's teeth he finds a small hole in one of them. This means that Jake needs to have a filling.

The dentist decides that Jake's tooth should be numbed. He rubs on some gum paste and gives him an injection.

Jake has a filling.

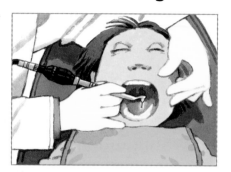

The dentist drills away the bad part of Jake's tooth. The dental nurse keeps it dry with a suction pipe.

Then she mixes a special paste to put into the hole. It is shiny and white.

Jake's filled tooth

This is what Jake's filled tooth looks like now.

The dentist presses the paste into the clean hole. Now Jake will not get a toothache.

61

The children learn how to look after their teeth.

Unhealthy teeth and gums look like this.

Healthy teeth and gums look like this.

The dentist shows them what will happen if they don't take care of their teeth properly.

Eat more of these.

Eat less of these.

He says they should be careful what they eat and drink because sugar and sweet foods and drinks are bad for teeth.

The dental nurse shows them how to brush their teeth really well. This gets rid of old food which can cause holes.

Jake and Jessie must brush their teeth twice a day with fluoride toothpaste to keep them clean and healthy.

Jake and Jessie go home.

On their way out, Mrs. Judd makes an appointment to see
the dentist for another check-up after six months.

The new baby

This is the Bunn family.

Mr. Bunn

Mrs. Bunn

Lucy
Bunn

Spock

Tom
Bunn

Bertie

Lucy is five and Tom is three. Mrs. Bunn is going to have a baby soon.

Granny and Grandpa come to stay.

They are going to look after Lucy and Tom when Mrs. Bunn is in the hospital. Lucy and Tom are excited to see them.

The Bunns get ready for the new baby.

There is a lot to do before the baby is born. Mr. and Mrs. Bunn decorate the baby's bedroom.

Lucy and Tom help too. Mrs. Bunn paints the bed for the baby to sleep in. Lucy uses the baby's bath to wash her doll.

69

Mrs. Bunn feels the baby coming.

Mrs. Bunn wakes up in the middle of the night. She thinks that the baby will be born very soon.

Everyone wakes up.

Mr. Bunn gets ready to take her to the hospital while
Grandpa phones to say that they are on their way.

The baby is born.

It is a little girl. Mr. and Mrs. Bunn are very happy. They are going to name her Susie.

Nurse Cherry weighs Susie to see how heavy she is, and measures her to see how long she is.

Susie is wrapped in a blanket. She has a name tag on her tiny wrist so she doesn't get mixed up with other babies.

As soon as Dad gets home, he tells Lucy and Tom all about their baby sister, Susie. They can't wait to see her.

They visit Susie.

The next day, Mr. Bunn takes Lucy and Tom to the hospital.
They are very excited to see their mother and baby sister.

74

Mrs. Bunn is in a room with two other mothers. They have new babies too. One of the mothers has twins.

The next day, Mrs. Bunn and Susie come home.

Mr. Bunn picks them up from the hospital. Everyone is excited and wants to hold the baby.

Susie goes to bed.

Susie is very sleepy. Mrs. Bunn is tired too. She will need a lot of help from Lucy, Tom and Mr. Bunn.

Mrs. Bunn feeds Susie.

When Susie is hungry, Mrs. Bunn feeds her with milk. Susie will need to be fed many times each day.

Susie has a bath.

Now it is time for Susie's bath. Mr. Bunn is very careful.
Lucy helps her Dad wash and dry Susie.

The Bunn family goes out.

Mr. and Mrs. Bunn, Lucy and Tom take Susie for a walk.
They are all very excited about the new baby.

Moving house

This is the Spark family.

Mr. Spark

Mrs. Spark

Sam
Spark

Peter

Sophie
Spark

Patch

Sam is seven and Sophie is five. They are moving into a
new house very soon.

This is the Sparks' old house.

They have sold it to Mr. and Mrs. Potts. The Potts have come today to measure the rooms.

The Sparks go to see their new house.

The house is being painted before the Sparks move in. Mr. Spark makes friends with the people who live next door.

Two men from Cosy Carpets arrive to put new carpets down in some of the rooms.

85

The Sparks pack up their old house.

It takes many days for Mr. and Mrs. Spark to sort out all of their things. Packing is hard work.

Sam makes sure that all of his things are packed too. But Sophie would rather play.

The Sparks move.

Frank

Bill

Early in the morning, a big truck arrives to take the Sparks' furniture to their new home.

88

Bess

REMOVA

Bill, and Frank and Bess, his helpers, load everything into the big truck. Then they drive it to the new house.

Everyone helps unload the truck.

Bill shows Sam and Sophie the inside of the truck. Then they all start to take the things into the new house.

They take things inside.

Bill, Frank and Bess carry the heavy furniture into the house. Mrs. Spark shows them where to put everything.

This is Sophie's new bedroom.

Dad helps Sophie to get it ready. He puts up the curtains.
Sophie is very excited about having a new room.

Sam has his own room too.

Sam likes the new house. Now he does not have to share a room with Sophie. Mrs. Spark helps him unpack.

The Sparks meet the people from next door.

In the afternoon the Sparks go for a walk down their street. There are lots of people to meet.

Mrs. Tobbit

Sophie and Sam have new friends to play with. Mrs. Tobbit from next door gives Mr. Spark a big cake to welcome them.

The Sparks go to bed.

Mr. and Mrs. Spark, Sophie and Sam are very tired after the move. They fall fast asleep in their new home.

The new puppy

This is the Appleby family.

Felix

Mr. Appleby

Mrs. Appleby

Amber Appleby

Ollie Appleby

Ollie and Amber are very excited. Today they are going to get their new puppy.

Dad drives them to Hazel Hill's house.

Eight weeks ago, Hazel Hill's dog, Gemma, had six tiny puppies. Ollie gives Gemma a pat.

Ollie and Amber go inside to see the puppies.

They are playing in the kitchen. Gemma looks protectively at her pups. "Which one should we choose?" says Ollie.

"They're all sweet," says Amber.

The smallest puppy runs up to Ollie and Amber. "I like this one best," says Ollie. "Me too," agrees Amber.

They are ready to go home.

Ollie carries the puppy to the car. "She's so little," says Amber, "let's call her Shrimp."

Shrimp meets Felix.

When they get home Ollie shows Shrimp her new bed.
But Shrimp is more interested in Felix, the cat.

They feed Shrimp.

"I think Shrimp's hungry," Ollie says to Amber. "Let's give her something to eat."

Ollie and Amber give Shrimp a bowl of water and some special puppy food. But Shrimp is much too excited to eat.

They take Shrimp outside.

Shrimp isn't allowed to go far until she has her injections.
Ollie and Amber play with her. Felix hides in the tree.

After supper, they put Shrimp to bed.

"Please can I sleep with her?" Amber asks her mother.
"No, you have your own bed, Amber," Mrs. Appleby says.

It's time for bed.

Mr. Appleby carries Amber upstairs. "Come on, sleepyhead," he says. "Goodnight, sleep tight, Shrimp," says Ollie.

The next day, Ollie and Amber get up early.

They want to see their new puppy right away. "Oh no,"
cries Amber. "What a mess!"

There is a big puddle on the floor.

Mrs. Appleby shows it to Shrimp. "Naughty girl," she says softly. Mr. Appleby gets something to clean it up.

Later, the Applebys take Shrimp to the vet.

Shrimp is very excited when she sees all the other animals.
She wants to play with them.

The vet gives Shrimp an injection.

"This won't hurt her!" The vet says. "It's just so that she will not catch any illnesses."

Amber and Ollie put Shrimp on a leash.

They take her out for a walk. "I love our new puppy,"
says Amber. "Me too," beams Ollie.

Going on a plane

Consultant: Jennifer Smith

This is the Tripp family.

Tim Tripp

Mr. Tripp

Mrs. Tripp

Rosie Tripp

Lily Tripp

Rover

Tim and Rosie are helping Mr. and Mrs. Tripp to pack.
They are going on a plane tomorrow.

They set off for the airport.

Grandpa Tripp takes them in his car. Lily is staying behind with Granny and Rover, the dog.

Mr. Tripp unloads their bags.

One of them topples over. It is Rosie's. She collects her things. "Sorry," says Mr. Tripp.

The Tripps check in.

"Here are the tickets," Mrs. Tripp says to the lady at the check-in counter. Another lady weighs their luggage.

The Tripps go through a metal detector.

Their bags go through an x-ray machine to make sure they are not carrying anything dangerous.

They board the plane.

A flight attendant shows them to their seats. Mr. Tripp puts their bags into a locker above their heads.

They're ready for take-off.

"Fasten your seat belts," says the flight attendant. "I've buckled Hippo in," says Rosie.

The plane takes off.

The pilot starts up the engines of the big plane. The flight attendant tells the passengers the safety rules.

The pilot waits for his turn to take off. Then the plane speeds down the runway and zooms up into the air.

It's time to eat.

"Here's your lunch," the flight attendant says to Mrs. Tripp. Another flight attendant gives Mr. Tripp a drink.

The flight attendant speaks to the pilots.

She goes into the cockpit and asks the pilots if they would like to have something to eat, too.

The plane will land soon.

Mrs. Tripp and Rosie go to use the toilet. Back in their seats, they listen to music on earphones.

Tim looks out of the window. "We're coming down," he shouts. Soon the plane lands safely on the runway.

The Tripps get off the plane.

They walk down the stairs to the bus that will take them to the airport building. "Catch my hat!" cries Mrs. Tripp.

They go through passport control.

PASSPORT CONTROL

An officer checks their passports. "Look," Rosie says to Mr. Tripp, "he's putting a big stamp in yours."

126

They collect their luggage.

They wait at the baggage carousel until their bags arrive.
"Here are my things," Rosie says to a porter.

127

The Tripps leave the airport.

Mrs. Tripp gives the porter some money. "Taxi, taxi," shouts Mr. Tripp. And off the Tripps go to their hotel!

Going to a party

This is the Dunn family.

Merry

Mr. Dunn

Mrs. Dunn

Nellie Dunn

Ned Dunn

Harvey

Nellie is five and Ned is three. Ned has a black and white puppy called Harvey.

A party invitation arrives.

Pete, the postman, gives Nellie a big letter. It is an
invitation to Larry White's party on Saturday.

They make fancy dress costumes.

Larry is having a fancy dress party. He wants all his
friends to come dressed as monsters.

Granny helps to make two monster costumes. But Grandpa is being a bit of a nuisance.

133

Nellie and Ned choose a present.

Mrs. Dunn takes Nellie and Ned to the toyshop to choose a present for Larry. Nellie wants to buy him a robot.

They are ready to go.

On Saturday Ned and Nellie get dressed in their costumes.
They are ready to go to the party.

They arrive at the party.

Nellie gives Larry his present. He is six years old today.
The cat is frightened of Ned.

Lots of other monsters have already arrived. They all try to guess who is wearing each mask.

Larry opens his presents.

All Larry's friends have brought him a present. He is very pleased with the robot from Nellie and Ned.

Mrs. White writes a list of who gave him each present.
He has lots of thank-you letters to write tomorrow.

There are lots of things to eat.

At last it is time to eat. Mrs. White has made all kinds of delicious things.

Larry has a chocolate birthday cake with a ghost on top.
Do you think he can blow out all his candles in one go?

They play party games.

After tea there are lots of games to play. It is Nellie's turn to pin the tail on the pig.

Ned wins first prize for the best fancy dress costume.
All the other monsters win prizes as well.

It's time to go home.

The party is over. It is time to go. Mr. Dunn comes to collect Nellie and Ned.

This edition published in 2002 by Usborne Publishing Ltd, Usborne House, 83-85 Saffron Hill, London EC1N 8RT, England.
Copyright © 2002, 1992, 1988, 1986, 1985 Usborne Publishing Ltd.
First published in America in 2003.
The name Usborne and the devices ♀ ⬤ are Trade Marks of Usborne Publishing Ltd.
All rights reserved. No part of this publication may be reproduced, stored in a retrieval system, or transmitted in any form or by any means
electronic, mechanical, photocopying, recording or otherwise, without prior permission of the publisher. Printed in China.